Giving

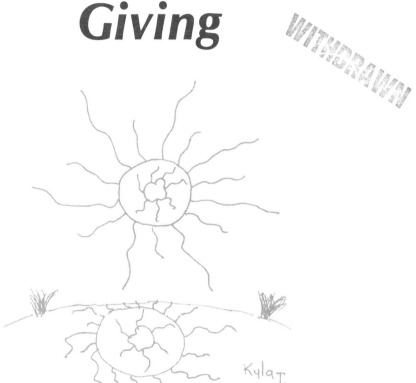

KylaT.

OJIBWA STORIES AND LEGENDS
FROM THE CHILDREN OF CURVE LAKE

Compiled & Edited by Georgia Elston

Published by
WAAPOONE
PUBLISHING & PROMOTION
Lakefield, Ont. K0L 2H0

Copyright © 1985 Curve Lake Band # 35

9TH PRINTING

Canadian Cataloguing in Publication Data

Giving: Ojibwa stories and legends from the children of Curve Lake

ISBN 0-9692185-0-8

1. Ojibwa Indians - Legends. * 2. Indians of North America - Ontario - Curve Lake - Legends. 3. Children's writings, Canadian (English) - Ontario. * 4. School prose, Canadian (English) - Ontario. * I. Elston, Georgia.

E99.C6G58 1985   398.2'08997   C85-090197-9

Design - Suzanne Wood
Printed by HOMESTEAD STUDIOS
Woodview, Ontario, Canada

CONTENTS

Stories and Legends

Illustrations

Pictures

Introduction

The stories and pictures in this book are a gift to you from the children of Curve Lake Reserve. Giving and sharing are important traditions of Canada's Native People — the *Anishinabe.

The hand shown on the cover is a symbol of honour, the promise in an agreement or treaty. Please accept this gift and its promise of enjoyment offered by these young Anishinabe.

For a long time the Anishinabe had no system for writing. They drew pictures on birchbark, carved them in rock, or told stories aloud. The strong voices of their old people, the elders, made them respected as story-tellers. As the Anishinabe moved from one hunting ground to another over thousands of years, so the stories and legends were carried with them in their minds.

When the Anishinabe led more settled lives, staying in one place on a reserve, they still liked to gather together to tell and listen to the old legends, just as their ancestors had on long cold winter nights in teepees, wigwams and lodges. They believed the meaning of life had been given to them by the Creator. It would never change and must be handed down in the legends from the elders.

If an Anishinabe child asks an older person a question, the answer is most often told in a story. It teaches something, but also entertains.

"Rain, rain go away"…"The north wind doth blow, and we shall have snow"…"Lady bug, lady bug, fly away home" are nursery rhymes told to white children, and recited back. Anishinabe children hear tales about nature too, because nature is so important to their people. Long ago their lives were spent seeking food and shelter from Mother Earth. They believed spirits lived in every part of Nature. The Creator told them to listen to the trees, the streams, the leaves, the animals. Anishinabe children are taught to understand and remember their strong ties to all living things.

*An-ish-i-naa-ba - "Original" or "first" man. Usually k or g is added to make it plural, but for this text Anishinabe is used instead of the general term "Indian."

5

Sometimes new stories would spring forth from a person's imagination. The Curve Lake children used their imaginations to create some of the stories in this book. That is also part of their custom.

Just as the Anishinabe believe in giving and sharing, they believe the earth, water, sky, birds and animals belong to everyone. Possessions are to be shared or given away to someone who needs them. The elders knew their people would always need the stories from their past.

Some of the elders will not tell legends until the first snow falls. They fear the spirits would be angry hearing themselves talked about. In the cold of winter the spirits were either far away or frozen under the snow.

The Anishinabe still respect this idea. One young Native man remembers a summer night of story telling in his village. On the way home, his faithful puppy was trotting along with him. Suddenly a bear confronted them. It ran off, but the man could still hear noises in the bush. Later, he was awakened to hear his dog, who slept outside under the steps, howling. When he got up the next morning, the pup was gone and bear tracks led back into the bush. They put out meat to trap the bear, and when it came it took seven shots to kill it. That young man says they never told stories in the summertime again.

Anishinabe parents still sometimes use legends and stories to get their children to behave. A bad spirit on a cold winter night makes the ice on the lake crack as he tries to get out. "Stop crying or he will get you!" you might be told.

Keeping quiet is important when you are hunting and tracking animals. Young Anishinabe are told stories while their parents wait for game. "You won't see any beaver, moose, or ducks if you are noisy."

Listening to stories teaches you to be quiet and pay attention. It trains you to hear other sounds of nature, as well as to be patient. A legend about how *Amik, the beaver, got his flat tail makes you really notice a lot about the beaver the next time you see one. Amik is a friend as well as a source of food and clothing.

*A-mík - Beaver

6

In the stories and legends, animals and people trade bodies. They all speak the same language, and all are part of the world of nature. They may help each other, or play tricks. The hero of a story is not all good, nor all bad. The Anishinabe enjoy hearing a funny story where ridiculous things happen.

Some of the legends may confuse the listener or reader because of sudden changes from human to animal. They may seem to have puzzling happenings. Legends often retell dreams which makes them seem bewildering. But they always convey a feeling of wonder, magic and mystery that the Anishinabe sense in nature.

The very first stories told were probably simple ones, about a hunt, a kill, a chase or a war. Then the story-tellers started to tell about their fears and hopes, or to explain acts of courage or cowardice. Later, ideas and beliefs were added. Religious beliefs, rules and laws, and humourous jokes were passed down "from the mouth" to become part of Anishinabe heritage.

Story-telling is sharing. The story-tellers are important, powerful members of the community. Anishinabe children respect their elders and learn from them. Because the stories are told over and over, listeners' memories are sharpened.

Many older Anishinabe were taught by the missionaries and white people that telling legends was not a good thing to do. This makes them shy and uncomfortable about telling them now. The young people need to seek out the old stories and tell their version of them so they are not lost for all time.

Legends explain by comparing nature with humanity. These comparisons, or metaphors, show that spirits, nature and humans are all one. Metaphors also make a lesson easier to remember.

Scenes from legends were some of the earliest Anishinabe art. In some of the children's drawings in this book you will see a circle. The circle has no beginning and no end. It goes on forever, just as do the sun, moon, earth and life. A circle inside a circle shows the soul in the middle with its body around it. The lines coming out from the body circle show our effect on the world around us. To the Anishinabe artist, lines show the power of relationships they see connecting everything.

The gift of these drawings from the Curve Lake children is their way of sharing their pictures of nature as well as their stories about it. The cover picture was given by Norman Knott, a well-known artist from Curve Lake.

Legends were made in the time when great things happened to start the Anishinabe traditions — when the land belonged to them. Those days are gone now, doomed by the coming of the white people. But listen quietly. Go back to a time when the land was quiet and the voices of nature could be heard. Let the children of the children of the elders of long ago tell their stories. Hush! Listen!

Georgia Elston

9

How the Birds Got Their Songs

from Michelle Whetung, age 12

Once the Great Spirit was walking through the forest when he heard joyous sounds coming from an Indian village. Still walking further on in the forest he heard nothing.

The next day he sent word by the squirrel to tell all the birds to gather in the big clearing. The next day as the Great Spirit walked into the clearing, he announced that the bird that flew the highest would get the most beautiful song.

The swallow's heart sank as he looked around him. The eagle would probably get the song. Suddenly, on impulse, he jumped into the eagle's nest and burrowed down and slept.

Later the swallow woke up. He looked around. There were hardly any birds, so up he flew. Soon the eagle tried to fly above him, and up went the swallow even higher.

As it turned out, he did get the prettiest song, but if you ever see a swallow, note how fast he flys to get away from the others.

How the Beaver Got Its Flat Tail
from Justin Knott, age 11

This story is about how mother beaver got her flat tail long, long ago. In those days, mother beaver and father beaver were deciding to have a baby, but first they had to repair the dam.

It was weak on one side and it needed more logs on the other side. That very day, mother beaver was far off cutting wood with her buck teeth. She didn't notice her tail was in the way of the tree she was chewing on.

Then CRASH, the tree landed right on her tail.

She was stuck there for a long, long time.

Then finally, some hunters came along. They saw the beaver was in pain, so they moved the tree. When the hunters saw her tail, they were surprised to see a beaver have a flat tail.

When mother and father beaver finished repairing their dam and had their baby, it had a flat tail too. And that's the story about how the beaver got its flat tail.

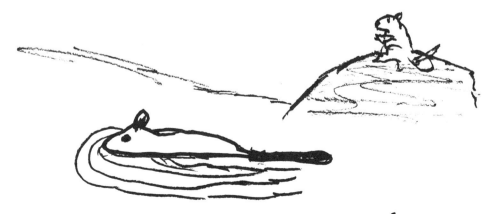

Russell Jacobs

TAMMY
TAYLOR

12

How the Indian Corn Got Its Colour

from Tammy Taylor, age 10

One day Nanabush did something very bad so the Spirit punished him. As Nanabush walked along, he fell into a pit full of different colours of paint.

He was angry, so angry that he tried looking for the Spirit who made him fall. He ran through fields and fields of corn.

And that's how Indian corn got its different colours.

The First Wolf

from Jason Redmond, age 10

Once there was a man who had two sons. They were down by the lake and the father was giving his sons lessons on their bows and arrows. When he finished, he told them not to go down to the lake without him because there was a Spirit man.

After they all left to go home, the sons came back to the lake, disobeying their father. They wanted to see who was better at shooting their bows and arrows. Then one shot his arrow so far that it landed in the Spirit man's canoe.

The Spirit man thought that this was a good way to get the boy in the canoe, and take him away. The Spirit man said, "Come and get your bow." The boy came out to his canoe and in a flash, the Spirit man grabbed him.

The other son saw this happening and ran home. When the father got to the lake, he looked across to the island and saw a wolf, not a boy. That's how the first wolf came to be.

How Nanabush Found Fire

from Richard Taylor, age 8

Nanabush went for a walk in the deep woods. He saw a chipmunk. The chipmunk said, "Where are you going?"

"I am going to look for some fire for my friends," said Nanabush.

"You have to go up that big mountain," said the Chipmunk. "Let me come with you, I want some fire too."

So the chipmunk and Nanabush went up the mountain together. Nanabush gave some fire to chipmunk and then he went home with some fire for his friends.

Why the Buffalo Always Looks Down

from Marcie Williams, age 12

One day Nanabush saw the buffalo running. He saw the buffalo stepping on the small baby animals. Nanabush did not like that, you see, because the buffalo looked up and could not see what they were doing.

So Nanabush grabbed a great big long stick and beat their necks. And Nanabush said, "Now you can see who you are running and stepping on."

And that's why the buffalo always looks down, and has a hump on his neck.

Tammy Taylor also gave a similar version of this story.

Why the Geese Fly in a V

from Leeann Pine, age 12

Nanabush was under water swimming, when he saw a flock of geese swimming above him. He got a rope and went under with it and tied the feet of the geese in a V.

When they went to fly, they flew in a V so they got used to it, and now they always fly in a V.

Duane
Jacobs

Kayla
Taylor

16

The Legend of Red Willow

from Kyla Taylor, age 11

One day when Nanabush was going to see his friend a long time ago, he scraped his arm on the thorn on a branch. He said, "Ow-w-w."

Then he saw that the thorn was stuck into him.

He kept going until he saw a bear caught in a trap. He stopped to help. Then the bear saw the cut and said, "Go ahead where you are going."

So Nanabush kept going and he thought to himself, "Should I leave my cut out in the fresh air?"

He did, and as he was walking his arm was scraping on the trees. When he got to the place where he was going to visit his friend, his blood was dried on the tree branches.

When he was coming home he saw what was on the trees. After that he called them Red Willow. The Red Willow was a good thing now for people.

How the Leaves Got Their Colours

from Gord Taylor, age 10

One fall day Nanabush decided to paint his wigwam. He had nice colours like red, orange, brown and green. Then one day a big storm came up and blew the paints all over the leaves.

When the wind stopped, Nanabush said to himself, "The colours look so nice that I will leave them there."

So that's why every fall the leaves change colours.

18

Amik and Wuzhuzk

from Michael Williams, age 8

One day Amik was swimming in the lake. And a Wuzhuzk came along. He wanted to swim, so he asked Amik.

"Yes, but only if you trade tails."

"Okay." Amik had an idea. He would keep Wuzhuzk's tail.

So they traded tails, and Amik didn't give back his tail. So that's why Amik has a big tail.

Mervin Jacobs and Richard Taylor also gave a similar version of this story.

Wa-sushk - Muskrat

Ryan Taylor

19

How the Bees Got Their Stingers

from Wendy Jacobs, age 9

Many, many years ago the bees had no stingers.

One day the bees came to Nanabush and said, "Nanabush, we need something to protect us. All the animals in the forest are taking our honey."

Then Nanabush decided that he would give the bees some stingers. Every day after that the bees could protect themselves and their honey.

The Baby and the Wolverine

from Sean Redmond, age 8

There once was an Anishinabe woman named Yellow Feather. All her life she had disobeyed her elders. Then one day she had a baby. It was a baby boy.

One day the elders said to the woman, "Don't leave your baby outside alone." But Yellow Feather did not listen. She took the baby outside and put him in the sandbox. Then she went to do the dishes.

Half an hour after he started to cry, but Yellow Feather said to herself that he was crying for nothing. But he was not.

Then he stopped. Then Yellow Feather went to get him, but he was gone. All that was there was a Wolverine and on his back was a shape of a baby. That is why not very long ago Wolverines had a back the shape of a baby.

The Talking Buckets

from Dawn Taylor, age 10

There was once an Anishinabe village that had only one well. One day an Anishinabe man went to get some water. When he got there, he thought he heard the buckets talking to each other.

He thought he heard one say, "I hate this job. All I do is go up and down all day."

The other bucket said, "I like this job because I know that so many people depend on me for water."

Then the other bucket said, "I suppose you're right."

Then they went on with their job.

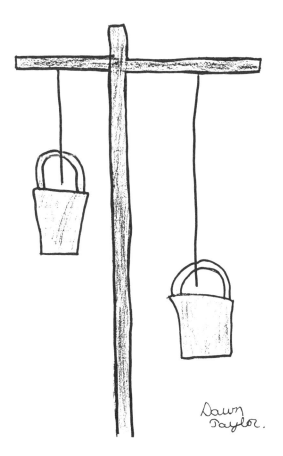

Dawn
Taylor.

Nanabush and Madamin

from Jeanette Knott, age 8

One hot summer day, a long time ago, Nanabush's people, the Anishinabe, ran out of food. So Nanabush had to go on a long journey. He paddled for many days and many nights. Then he reached the island where stood Madamin.

Madamin said, "If you want food for your people, you will have to fight me three times."

So Nanabush said, "Okay."

They started to fight. When they were done that day, Nanabush and Madamin rested. The next day Nanabush went back to the island. He fought Madamin again. Both times Nanabush beat Madamin.

Before Nanabush left the island that night, Madamin said, "Tomorrow if you beat me, I want you to bury me."

The third day, Nanabush beat Madamin.

Madamin said, "Now take off my husks."

So Nanabush took off his husks and when he was done, he buried Madamin.

When Nanabush came back the next day, he watered him. Madamin started to grow. He grew into a corn plant, and that's how we got corn.

A similar version of this story was given by Mervin Jacobs.

Ma-dá-min - corn (seed, food of wonder)

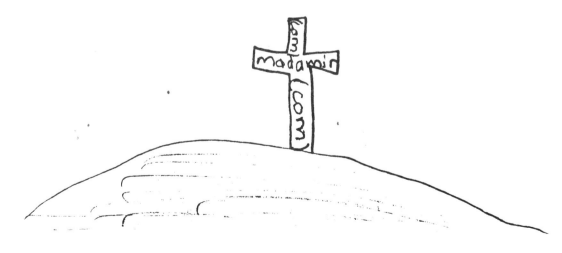

Dawn Taylor

24

How the Racoon Got His Mask

from Jason Redmond, age 10

One day a racoon was looking for some food. He found an old tree which had some honey in it. The racoon was so hungry he never washed his paws. His paws were all black and dirty.

The racoon ate a lot of honey and his paws were stuck in the honey. After a while he got his paws loose. The racoon wiped his eyes but all the while he was making black rings around his eyes.

Just then a bear came along. He looked in the tree for the honey he hid there. It was all gone. He was mad!

The bear looked at the racoon and grabbed him. The bear had very muddy paws and rubbed them on the racoon's eyes. The bear thought that the racoon's tail looked bare so he made rings around the racoon's tail.

This tells us that the rings around his eyes and tail mean the racoon is a thief.

The Anishinabe of Curve Lake Reserve

Long, long ago the Anishinabe came over frozen water far in the north. These people travelled great distances over the country until they reached a land of plenty. After many ages, a great darkness fell over their land. When at last a bright light was seen, it turned out to be a mountain of water. Only a few of the people lived after it passed over them. These chosen Anishinabe built a big canoe and were saved.

A new earth was formed after the mountain of water passed and the Anishinabe were helped to survive and thrive by their great spirit, Nanabush. Their traditions were formed to be handed down through the generations.

As the Anishinabe continued to roam the land, fishing, trapping, hunting and growing some crops in summer, they lived in partnership with nature. This was not to last forever.

After thousands of years, they saw the first white people. These were mostly Jesuit priests, sent from Europe as missionaries. The Jesuits met some of the Anishinabe in villages on the north shore of Lake Huron. They had fisheries at the mouths of rivers teeming with fish. About this time, the Anishinabe in this area were given the name Ojibwa.

The Ojibwa were at war with the Iroquois and kept driving the Iroquois south out of the Ojibwa hunting grounds. By 1740 the Iroquois were defeated and the Ojibwa tribes controlled most of the land that is now south-eastern Ontario. The Mississaga Ojibwas had driven the Mohawks (the chief tribe of the Iroquois) down the valley of the Otonabee River. They defeated them at the battle place called Nogojiwanong (meaning "place at the end of the rapids") which was to become the city of Peterborough. Rather than have the two tribes fight each other to death, the elders arranged a treaty so that peace between the two would be assured forever.

26

Many of the Eastern Ojibwa, or Mississagas, stayed to hunt and fish and trap in the Kawartha Lakes area. It is their descendants who now live at Curve Lake. They are of the Crane and Eagle clans.

As European settlers began flooding into this part of the country the government bought the land cheaply from the Anishinabe. In forty years, millions of acres were sold for pennies an acre and annual presents. Sometimes the Anishinabe thought they were putting the land in the King's hands for safe-keeping, until they needed it.

The Anishinabe had no idea what "owning" land meant. They didn't fight each other for possession of land. They fought to keep control over what was growing or living on it.

They were used to moving their villages to better hunting grounds, or because they were defeated in a battle. They felt the land still belonged to all.

The Mississagas settled into the valley of the Otonabee River, and as far east as Brockville along the St. Lawrence River. One small band left Balsam Lake because the water there was too rough for their canoes, dug out of tree trunks.

Their scouts reported an island with water on three sides. They gathered on the shore of Little Mud Turtle Lake, later to be called just Mud Lake. Here their canoes could be kept handy to the shore for a fast get-away from enemies. The elders preferred to have water all around them so the white people would not build so close to them.

This Kawartha Lakes region was forested with red and white pine trees, sugar maples, oak, basswood, elm, aspen, ash, beech and white birch. It was rich in game, birds and fish.

As the government sold this land they had bought so cheaply from the Anishinabe to European settlers, they set some of it aside, reserved it, for the Native People. The settlers cleared land, built homes and farmed. It became harder and harder for the Anishinabe to hunt and fish, or even move around far off the reserves. The forests were being chopped down and the fur trade was declining.

The government also granted a tract of land to the New England Company, a group of missionaries, in 1832. This tract was 1600

acres on Mud Lake. The missionaries began gathering together the Mississagas in the area, to live on this parcel of land.

At first only a dozen or so families moved there. Soon, though, the excellent fishing, hunting, wild rice, maple sugar and cranberries attracted others. The missionaries began to move the people from their wigwams into houses. A church, school and a teacher's residence were also built.

With less and less uncultivated land, and poorer hunting and fishing, life on the reserves was not always happy, but gradually they accepted the settled life over the old wandering ways.

The Anishinabe did not take to farming as quickly as the missionaries had hoped. It took over twenty years before they really began to plant and grow crops as serious farmers. In 1857 they raised spring wheat, Indian corn, potatoes and hay.

Some of the men worked in nearby lumber camps. They began to make wooden canoes instead of ones dug out of logs. The women wove sweetgrass baskets and made decorative items of beadwork and porcupine quills.

By now they were more aware of the European way of regarding land as a possession. Two of the Curve Lake leaders, John Irons and Daniel Whetung complained to the government that the Mississagas were discouraged because the New England Company could sell and put them off this land at any time.

Near the beginning of the 19th century, the government paid the missionary company for this land out of the money they would have paid that year to the Mississagas. Thus, this band of Anishinabe had to pay for a small part of the country they had once owned entirely. The federal government held the land in trust for the Anishinabe.

When the New England Company missionaries left, the members of the Mud Lake Band ran the community. The Mississagas had not always had chiefs — only respected elders whom they listened to and followed. Now they elected chiefs and council members. They decided who would be church sexton, organist, bush ranger, constable and school teacher. Decisions were made by consulting with the community.

The people of Mud Lake may not have been rich by European standards, but they looked after themselves and led lives of satisfaction. The constable enforced their laws. For bad language or behaviour, a fine had to be paid. Children under 14 could not be out after 8 p.m. in the winter and 9 p.m. in the summer.

Mud Lake was still a small community that could only be reached by water. In the 1800s a ferry began to cross back and forth from the wharf at Jack Whetung's point to Ennismore. It was rowed by oars. In 1833 Mud Lake became known as Chemong, from the Ojibwa cheemanu, or "canoe", and the reserve became Chemong Village. In 1915, a ferry using a chain-cable and crank could carry a horse and buggy across. Five years later, a road from the reserve through the forest was built, to join the main highway to Peterborough.

Hunting and trapping were no longer the main business. In 1927 the children of Curve Lake were prohibited from even using catapults.

These things really changed life at Chemong Village. Young people could go to schools off the reserve. Electricity brought modern living to the Anishinabe. In 1963 the reserve's name was legally changed to Curve Lake Reserve.

Today Curve Lake is like many small towns, except that when you pass the sign that welcomes you to the reserve, you actually leave the Province of Ontario. The reserves in Canada are the responsibility of the Federal Government in Ottawa.

The Anishinabe of Canada are divided into 559 groups, called Bands. The residents of Curve Lake Reserve belong to Band #35. The reserves are all different sizes and band members do not have to live on their reserve. About 750 Mississagas live at Curve Lake.

Children at Curve Lake go to school on the reserve up to Grade 4. There is also a daycare centre for the very young and a junior and senior kindergarten. Yellow school buses take older pupils into the village of Lakefield for grades 3 to 13.

The Ojibwa language is taught in the Curve Lake day school. So many English words have no meaning in Ojibwa. There is no word for glove, but nees-kee-min-jee-cow-an means "a mitt that spreads." Anishinabe is the word Native People use for themselves. It means "original" or "first man" and translates as "people."

Young people at Curve Lake get together regularly, once a week after school to learn their native crafts, language, customs, legends and music. They take part in the annual Pow-wow to which many visitors come. They have a ball diamond and often go camping on Fox Island on Buckhorn Lake. When the lake is frozen they have a skating rink on their shore. The fields and woods all around on the reserve give them freedom to run and play in the natural environment. They can hunt and fish close to their homes.

Many of their parents work in the home, or in nearby buildings, making native craft items. The children learn these skills of basket weaving, beadwork, moccasin sewing just by seeing it done regularly around them. They take great pride in their cultural traditions.

They have many of the same interests as white children, but a richness is added to their lives from their Anishinabe heritage.

Georgia Elston

How the Lady Slipper Came to Be

from Alison Williams, age 12

An Ojibwa tribe was camping where Sieux Lookout is now. The tribe was slowly starving. The Medicine Man told them to follow the setting sun. The chief said, ''We shall go next moon!''

The chief had a daughter who was a year old.

It was time to leave and the chief and his wife got ready. The tribe left that day. They walked and walked the rest of the day. When they were going to rest, the chief and his wife were looking for their girl. They never found her.

The chief and some warriors went back and all they found was her moccasin. They buried it.

The next year when they came back to the grave, they found a lady slipper plant growing there.

Marcie Williams, Stacey Lynn Jacobs and Christina Taylor also gave a similar version of this story.

The Legend of Tamarack and Chickadee

for Cameron Pine, age 5
(by his mother, B. Pine)

The Anishinabe say that long ago the tamarack was evergreen, like the red pine. They say its beautiful green, cone-shaped form graced the forest all through the long winter.

One day, during a terrible storm, a chickadee was injured. It was nearly dead from cold. The little bird struggled through the blowing snow until it stood at the foot of a tall tamarack.

"I need your help. Please drop some of your lower branches to shelter me from the storm," the little bird begged.

"I should say not," tamarack quickly replied. "I did not grow beautiful green branches to break them off for you. I'm sorry, but I prefer to keep my fine form."

So the chickadee pulled its small battered body to the foot of a tall red pine. "Please drop some of your lower branches to shelter me from the storm," the bird cried.

The red pine pitied the poor little chickadee. Quickly it dropped enough branches to shelter the bird. Now the Great Spirit saw what had happened and said to the red pine, "You will always drop your lower branches to remind others that you paid a high price so a small bird could live."

When tamarack heard this, he was glad he had not dropped any branches. "Now," he thought, "I will keep my fine form."

"Yes, tamarack," the Great Spirit said, "you will keep your fine form, but from today your needles will begin to turn brown. You will soon die and be forgotten because you had no mercy for a chickadee."

The tamarack wept, "The punishment is too harsh," he cried.

Chickadee had crept out from under the red pine branches lying on the snow. He pitied tamarack.

"Oh, Great Spirit," the bird said. "Please don't let tamarack die and be forgotten."

"Very well," the Great Spirit said to chickadee.

Turning to tamarack he said, "You will not die and be forgotten. But every autumn you will lose your fine green needles and stand naked all winter as a reminder to others that it is better to have mercy and be kind than to be vain and selfish."

Joanne
Pine

How Nanabush Lost His Eyes

from Leslie Shilling, age 9

Many moons ago, Nanabush didn't have anything to do, so he went out looking for somebody to play with. After many hours of a trip, he found six ducks. They were throwing their eyeballs up, so Nanabush asked if he could play.

They said, "Okay," so he started playing. It was such fun that he threw his eyes so high they never came down.

He went into the forest and all the trees laughed at him but the pine tree. The pine said, "Use some of my gum."

"Okay," said Nanabush. He rolled the gum into circles. Then he had eyes again.

Leslie Shilling

How the Racoon Got Rings on Its Tail

from Christina Taylor, age 8

It was a hot day and Nanabush wanted to go and visit his two old friends. They were both blind. Nanabush had made a rope for the two blind men to follow to the river to get a bucket of water whenever they were thirsty. This day, they put four pieces of meat in a pot to cook before they went for water.

While they were doing that, a racoon was looking for some mischief. When he saw them leaving to follow the rope with two buckets in their hands, he sneaked past the two old men and went right to the teepee and stole two pieces of meat. He gobbled them up and left.

He left just in time because the two old men were coming back. When they got there, they went straight to the pot with the meat in it. One old man didn't get any because the racoon ate it. He didn't know that, so he blamed it all on his other blind friend. He was so mad he started punching him and slapping him.

While they were fighting, the racoon took one end of the rope and hid it in the bushes and waited and waited and waited.

Finally they came out to get water again and the racoon started to giggle. The men felt their way to the other end of the rope and all they could feel was grass and thistles.

The men yelled, "Hey, where's the water? What happened?"

Nanabush arrived and saw the racoon. He went into the bush and pulled out the racoon by the ear. Nanabush said, "You need a punishment."

So Nanabush painted rings on his tail. And he moved the rope back to the river where it was supposed to be.

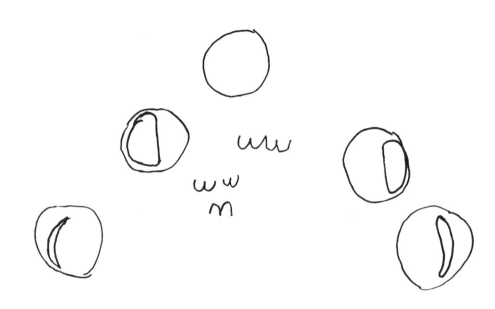

Beay
taylor

38

The Five Moons of Winter

from Beau Taylor, age 7

Once long ago the animals in the forests were wondering how many moons there should be in winter. Bull Moose said, "There should be as many moons as there are hairs on my body."

The other animals said that would be too long. "We would have snow and cold all the time."

Amik spoke up next. He said there should be as many moons of winter as there are scales on his tail. That would still be too long. Wee-sa-kay-jac said it would still be too long to survive in the cold.

Little Makikii, the frog spoke up and said, " I here should be as many moons as I have toes." All the animals told little Makikii to be quiet. Wee-sa-kay-jack decided this was a good length of time for winter. From then on we have five moons of winter – November, December, January, February and March.

This story was also given by Gale Nodin Knott.

Mú-ku-kee - frog

Why the Ice Cracks

from Beau Taylor, age 7

Have you ever heard the ice crack when it is really clear, cold, and crisp out and there is no snow on the ice?

Long ago the Anishinabe used to say that Windego was trapped under the ice. The cracking was made by Windego banging his head on the ice trying to get out. The Anishinabe would always see the cracks he made.

Windego was never able to break through and was always trapped under the ice until the spring thaw.

Wiń-da-goh - a spirit, the glutton

How the Leaves Change Colour

from Thomas Jacobs, age 9

One day Nanabush was walking in the woods to get some berries to make dye so he could paint his wigwam. He was nearly home when he saw a baby bird who had fallen out of its nest.

He picked it up and started up the tree. He was almost to the nest when he spilled his dyes all over the leaves. He then told the leaves that they looked pretty and he would come every fall to throw dye all over them.

How the Chipmunk Got Its Stripes

from Ryan Taylor, age 11

Long ago when the earth was young, a Little Red Chipmunk (which had no stripes) was playing with Little Running Bear. At this, the great Spirit Manitou, was happy. He wasn't always happy because sometimes the animals fought amongst each other.

But when he saw the two playing he was happy.

Little Running Bear was happy too, because he and the Chipmunk were having fun. When Little Running Bear went home, Little Red Chipmunk got lonely, so he decided to get into mischief.

So he went into a big cave, and you know what he saw?

He saw a great Big Bear. And he chirped and chattered as loud and as hard as he could. He scared the Big Bear so much that his fur almost flew off. When the Big Bear saw that it was the Little Chipmunk that had scared him, he was so mad he scratched the Chipmunk's back.

The next day the Chipmunk saw a female Chipmunk and she saw the scratches on his back. She nursed him back to health and they had a family one year later. And all the little Chipmunks had scratches like their father.

And that's how the Chipmunk got stripes.

How the Bear Got a Short Tail

from Stephanie Jacobs, age 9

Many moons ago Brother Bear was sitting by a tree and Brother Fox passed by with six fish.

Brother Bear asked, ''Where did you get those fish?''

Brother Fox said, ''Down at the pond.''

Brother Bear said in a puzzled voice, ''But it's winter.''

Brother Fox said, ''I went ice fishing. I cut a hole in the ice, stuck my tail in and the fish would bite my tail.''

Brother Bear headed on down the road to the pond. He cut his hole and stuck his tail in the hole. He waited and waited. Then his tail stung and stung. But still he sat.

Then it really stung. So he pulled. But his tail would not come out. He could not get up.

Then he pulled really hard and finally got out. And there was no fish on the end of his short tail. Fox laughed and laughed. And Bear went home sad.

A similar version of this story was given by Jeanette Knott, Kyla Taylor and Bryan Taylor.

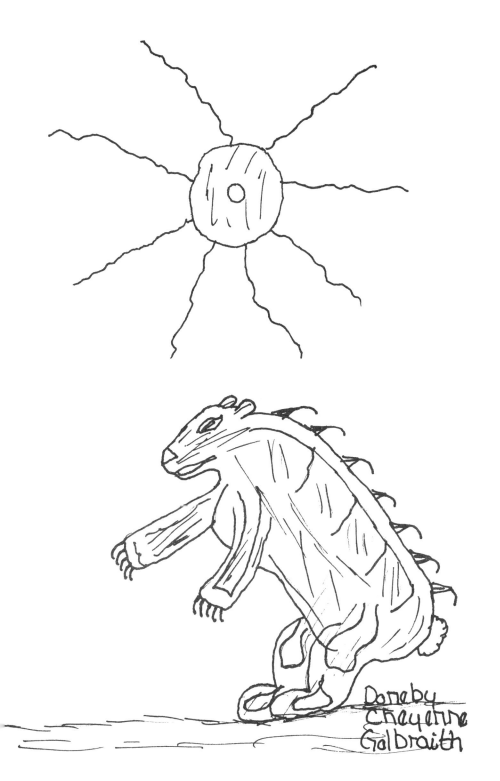

Done by
Cheyenne
Galbraith

43

How the Turtle Set the Animals Free

from Autumn Watson, age 7

Eagle was the fastest of all animals so he was chief. One night Turtle had a dream. He was told to race Eagle, win the race, and set the Animal people free from Eagle's rule.

Turtle made a plan. He told Eagle to carry him up into the air, to drop him and whoever reached the ground first would win.

Eagle took Turtle high up in the sky and dropped him. Turtle fell like a rock. He won the race. The Animals were happy.

This means you can do anything you put your mind to.

How Food Was Given

from Autumn Watson, age 7

Long ago the Animal and Plant people had to find out how the Anishinabe would live and what they would eat.

The four chiefs, Bear, Salmon, Root and Berry decided to give themselves and their people as food.

This means that everyone can help one another.

Autumn does not live at Curve Lake, but she visits there often.

How the Birch Bark Got Its Marks

from Tammy Taylor, age 11

One day Nanabush, the Great Spirit, was out exploring when he heard noises coming from the forest. He looked around and saw the birch and the spruce quarrelling.

"Mr. Spruce, I'm nicer and more gentle than you. My white body attracts all the Anishinabe and they come and get some of my white, smooth body for their teepees. And they look at you as if they don't really care. You're green and prickly," said the lovely birch tree.

Nanabush saw what was going on, so he tore a branch off the Spruce and started hitting the birch tree.

"Caw! Caw! No! No!" cried the birch tree.

Ever since the birch is no longer king of the forest for he has scars all over his white, smooth body.

A similar version of this story was also given by Gaylord Knott.

Caw - No

DRAWN
BY
TAMMY
TAYLOR

How the Rosebush Got Its Thorns

from Tammy Taylor, age 11

Many years ago all rosebushes were very sad because the birds and bees would eat their sweet centres out. One day as Nanabush was out walking in the woods, he, the Nishnaabe spirit of all kind, heard a weeping sound. But he did not know where it came from.

He looked to the left and then to the right. When he looked to the right he noticed a whole bush of roses with tears in their eyes. He felt hurt. He walked up to the roses and said, "What is your reason for crying?"

"Well, you see, the birds and bees eat our centres out," replied the rosebushes.

"For how long?" asked Nanabush.

"Long enough," said the chief of the rosebushes angrily.

"Well, well, well," said Nanabush in a rough voice. "May I be any help?"

"Well ... I guess so," said the rosebushes' chief.

Nanabush said he would meet them there the next morning.

The night went very slowly. Nanabush awoke very early that morning. He headed out to the field. When he reached the rosebushes the sun was just rising over the field.

Nanabush looked to find the roses. There they were waiting for him. He ran over with thorns in his hand and put them gently on the roses. They didn't know how to thank him.

No longer did the birds and bees eat their sweet centres out.

The Star

from Stacey Lynn Jacobs, age 11

One night two men were sitting beside a tree when all of a sudden they saw a falling star.

One of the men said, "Look!"

They went to where the star had fallen. The star said, "May I stay here by the water where you can see me?"

In the morning the two men said, "Let's go and see the falling star." So the men went to the water where the star had fallen, but all they could see was a water lily.

How the Rabbit Got Its Long Ears

from Duane Jacobs, age 11

A long time ago a man named Nanabush went for a walk and the bad little rabbit followed him. The bad little rabbit played very mean tricks on Nanabush.

Nanabush saw the rabbit. He chased him but the rabbit was too fast. Then Nanabush sat under a tree. The rabbit saw him and played some more tricks on Nanabush.

Nanabush got so mad that he ran faster than the rabbit. They ran all over the bush. Then Nanabush caught him by the ears and pulled on them so hard they became bigger, and that's how the rabbit got his long ears.

The Loon's Necklace

from Rachel Whetung, age 9

Once long ago, an old blind man lived in a hut beside the forest with his family. Oh, how he longed to see again.

One day his son and his wife went to the next village to trade some skins for food because they were starving.

They would not be back until next week. While they were gone, the man became very hungry. Before he became blind, he had been the Shaman. So the old man took his magic rattle and went to the mountain.

"Oh, Great Spirit," he called. "What do I have to do to have my sight back?"

"Go to my brother the loon. He will help you," said the Spirit.

So the old man went as quickly as he could to the marsh, because his family would be back in three days. He travelled one day. When he reached the marsh, he sat down on the shore and sang a sad song.

Then he sat and listened. Then he heard the call of a loon.

"What is it you want?" asked the loon.

"I wish to see again," answered the man.

"Then grab hold of my wings and dive under the water with me."

The old man did as he was told and when they came up, the loon asked, "Can you see?"

"No," answered the man, "not like I should."

Then the loon said, "Then dive with me again."

So he did. When they came up, the old man said. "I can see! Oh, thank you, loon!"

The man took off his shell necklace. He threw it to the loon. It landed on his neck. It broke and shells fell on the loon's back. Now the loon was happy with his shell necklace.

It only took the rest of the day for the old man to walk back. He shot two deer. When his family came back, the old man told them what had happened. They had a feast and ate the two deer. They were never hungry again.

This story was also given by Justin Knott and Holly Payton

DONE BY
Marcie William

The First Bow and Arrow

from Joanne Pine, age 9

Long ago a young Anishinabe hunter set out to find a bear. As he peeked through the bushes, he saw a big black bear. The big black bear was feasting on grapes off the vines.

The young hunter crawled very close, close enough that he could almost touch the bear. He quickly raised his spear for the death stroke, but just then his foot slipped.

He almost fell under the bear's claws. The bear turned and started for the hunter. The hunter regained his balance and aimed the spear.

It caught on a twisted grapevine which was clinging to an ash sapling. He jerked on the sapling. It bent, sending the spear quickly through the air, and into the bear's neck.

The furry animal gave a few last kicks and died. The excited hunter tried the sapling and the vine again. He had just made the first bow and arrow.

How Land Came to Be

from Jessica Knott, age 6

A turtle had a big shell. He turned it into land. Everything grew there – trees and flowers and animals and grass. And that is how land came to be.

Done By
Marcel
Williams

Acknowledgments

When Brenda Neill asked me to edit some stories written by her Grade Five class at Ridpath Junior Public School in Lakefield, little did I know it would lead to this book.

The children were writing legends as well, as part of a unit on Native Studies. Since many of the pupils came from Curve Lake Reserve, a collection of Native legends and stories from all the children of Curve Lake seemed a natural project.

Thanks to the co-operation of Larry Axcell, principal, and his staff, I began working with the Native children at the school. As the work progressed, I had the good fortune to meet Wilma Taylor, Native Studies Co-ordinator at Curve Lake. Wilma was my right arm throughout the project, and I owe her a great debt of thanks.

We included as well the Grade Seven and Eight pupils at Lakefield Intermediate School who came from Curve Lake. Their principals, Jim Northey and Gary Sutherland, and the staff, were also most co-operative. The Grade One and Two pupils at the Curve Lake Day School under the direction of Leona Toulouse, their teacher, contributed stories and pictures too.

As the project grew, a grant from the Canada Council seemed a possibility. The application was accepted and producing this book as a professional publication became a reality.

The kids were great! They had all kinds of enthusiasm and interest. They also produced the marvellous illustrations seen on these pages, mostly in one main art session. It is their book and they are the ones to be congratulated for its existence.

When Norman Knott, the well-known artist from Curve Lake, came along to help the children with their drawings, he offered the use of one of his paintings for the cover. He even was responsible

55

for the title, *Giving*. Norman had originally entitled this painting, "Alone" but said he had always wished he had called it "Giving." Since the children were giving the stories and legends in the book, Norman felt that was an appropriate title. And so, to Norman, my thanks for both his generosity and inspiration.

The School Committee of Curve Lake was most co-operative in supporting my ~~work, and a committee of Leona Toulouse,~~ Wreathia Williams ... ~~ough~~ to read over the st...... ... they were ......

Mel Jacobs, then Manager for the Peterborough area of Indian and Northern Affairs, also took time from a busy schedule to read over the material I had written for inclusion.

Having Suzanne and Don Wood of Homestead Studios in this area to print the book was a stroke of luck. I knew of their work on other children's books from my days in educational publishing in Toronto and felt safe in their hands. They did not let me down.

My classmates and professors in Native Studies 384 at Trent University added their input for which I am most grateful. The native students were generous with their time in talking to me, and John Milloy, Greg Conchelos and their assistant Rodney Bobiwash helped instil some scholarly aspects in my work.

My family cannot be left out. My daughter, Heather, was a big help with double-checking and some bright ideas as well. My son, Harold, although deep in his law studies, gave me heartening encouragement and sage suggestions. The business acumen and support of Jake, my husband, are also much appreciated.

The ABC's boil down to Acknowledging Brenda for starting me on this work, Canada Council for funding it, and the Children for making it possible.

Giving became the first publishing venture for Waapoone Publishing and Promotion. It has shown the way for future books, but none could provide the glow and thrill to compare with that of working with the children of Curve Lake.

Georgia Elston